$2 \dfrac{95}{T}$

CONFLICT AND UNDERSTANDING IN MARRIAGE

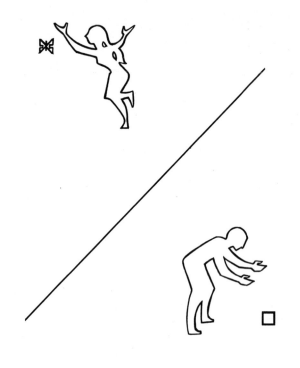

CONFLICT

AND

UNDERSTANDING

IN

MARRIAGE

Paul Plattner

TRANSLATED BY JOHN R. BODO

Foreword by Paul Tournier

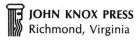 **JOHN KNOX PRESS**
Richmond, Virginia

To My Wife

This book is a translation of *Glücklichere Ehen*, © copyright by Verlag Hans Huber, Bern 1950.

Standard Book Number: 8042-1093-4
Library of Congress Catalog Card Number: 79-93831
© M. E. Bratcher 1970
Printed in the United States of America

FOREWORD
to the American Edition

It is a pleasure to introduce Dr. Paul Plattner to American readers. He is a psychiatrist and for the past twenty years has directed a well-known private clinic at Münchenbuchsee near Bern, Switzerland. Dr. Plattner is a psychoanalyst connected with the Zurich school of C. G. Jung and Alphonse Maeder. He serves as a marriage counselor in Bern and has directed a "*Groupe Balint,*" a course in which medical practitioners receive psychoanalytic training in order better to understand and care for their patients and also better to understand themselves and their relationships with their patients.

Dr. Plattner has also worked closely with me in organizing the annual sessions on the "medicine of the person" since their beginning in 1947; these sessions are called "the Bossey Conferences," for the Ecumenical Institute where the meetings are often held. He is the one who gave us the slogan I have often cited: "The medicine of the person begins with the person of the doctor himself." ("*La médicine de la personne commence par la personne du médicin lui-même.*") This means that we are not able to help our patients attain the full humanity which we call the "person" unless we have experienced it in our own personal life. Dr. Plattner has been a strong support for me and a faithful friend during difficult times in my own life. Furthermore, he has introduced our concept of medicine in the clinic he directs.

Moreover, a report which Dr. Plattner gave for one of our sessions at Bossey was the starting point of this book. Doctors of all specialties who are interested in the medicine of the person are astounded by the effect of marriage difficulties on the health of their patients. In the absence of psychological training, doctors very often do not know how to help patients overcome their difficulties. Physicians are sometimes embarrassed by their own difficulties in marriage, and they may suffer secretly from the striking contrast between the brilliant success of their professional careers and a certain feeling of failure in their marriages. Their wives are able to sense this also. They say, for example, "You are able to help everyone but me—you don't know how to help me." My American friends will be amused to learn that in his report at Bossey Dr. Plattner used my wife and me as examples so that the doctors, who know us well, could understand better what he was saying. They all knew that I was an orphan and that during my studies and at the beginning of my marriage and my career, I had become an example of the "thought-type" (Denktypus) by the repression of my "affective function" (Gefühlsfunktion), but that my wife, on the contrary, mistrusted her intellectual ability and had repressed this function while developing her affections.

Dr. Plattner then explained how our marriage had led each of us to our "integration." In other words, our marriage caused us to develop our repressed functions—

thought, for my wife, and affective sensibility, for myself
—so well that all my career from then on has been gov-
erned by my experiences of personal contact. This was
to show that marriage restored an important function for
the personal development of each of the marriage partners.

In all this, Dr. Plattner, as he said himself, followed
closely the teachings of C. G. Jung, and I think that this
will interest American readers, because, it seems to me,
this master is less known than Freud in the United States.
Everyone knows that the two pioneers worked together
like brothers at the beginning of psychoanalysis and that
the two of them separated in tears when Freud was not
able to admit that spiritual and teleological factors entered into play alongside the instinctive factors in the
human soul. But Freud and Jung always held each other
in the greatest esteem and loyally abstained from all
polemic against each other.

This book will be of interest to the specialists—
psychiatrists, psychologists, marriage counselors, and
churchmen—who in the United States are better able
to understand than in Europe the help that psychology
is able to bring in the exercise of their ministry. I also
think that the quite practical characteristics of psychology please Americans, who are all animated with such
zeal for helping other people. Though this book is closely
related to the doctrines of C. G. Jung, it is by no means
pedantic, but is marked above all by the personal experience that the author has acquired during a long career
and by his ability to make lucid, friendly, and compre-
hensive observations.

But I hope that this book will especially interest couples who want to make their marriage more complete and happy. There are very many who, without being in serious conflict, are more or less disappointed, without knowing why. I am inclined to describe what happens by the phrase "phenomenon of the siphon." When someone puts a siphon at the outlet of a reservoir, the reservoir is able to fill up silently for a long time. When it is full, the siphon primes itself, and all the accumulated liquid flows out with a rush. In the same way, a married couple is able to live for long periods without an uproar. They certainly have critical opinions about each other. But by generosity, by goodwill, by religious ideals perhaps, they bypass these opinions and avoid expressing them in order not to hurt each other. They are themselves often proud of bearing with each other this way without saying anything.

But one day a somewhat hasty reproach slips out from one of the marriage partners; abruptly the siphon primes itself. The other partner suddenly feels that his spouse doesn't understand; he is distressed, hurt, annoyed—he makes a sharp retort. By an automatic psychic mechanism, all sorts of incidents from the past surge tumultuously into his mind. And then both of them hurl at each other the old griefs which had seemingly been forgotten. Carried away by this aggressive outburst, they are both able to say biting words which they will later regret, but which will remain, in turn, like wounds. Dialogue is set in motion, but in a destructive way.

Then several hours later, when this passionate outburst has passed, when they are burdened with guilt feelings, both of them agree on one thing: that the object of their quarrel appears trifling—sometimes they aren't even able to remember what the argument was about! Now is the time when dialogue is needed—constructive dialogue. It is necessary to see what was true in the offensive words and exaggerations that they have exchanged. But now because the passion has died down, the two have nothing more to say to each other. Or, if they speak, it is so vague that it means nothing, and that leaves them uneasy, as if the injuries they sustained were ridiculous. It is as if they were speaking not of themselves but of a third party, and they are a little ashamed of expressing such trivial criticisms. And so this deceptive peace continues until the next crisis.

It is at this very moment that the reading of this book is able to initiate between the two partners a truly constructive dialogue. They see, in effect, that there is certainly a problem to resolve, a real problem of the adaptation of their respective types, and that it is much more important than they think during their good periods and less serious than they feel during their moments of anger. This will encourage them to open themselves up to each other in a deeper way. Of course, they will both be tempted to use this book to justify themselves against the criticisms which they feel the other is bringing against them. "You see: you are always reproaching me for my behavior; it's described here—it's because I am an extrovert while you're an introvert!" But they will be able also to use this book in order to try to understand each other better, to truly accept their differences in type and in reactions, and not merely bear with them.

The marriage dialogue will be fruitful when each looks at himself and seeks for his own responsibility instead of blaming the other. And then each of the partners will be stimulated in his personal development; he will be able to grow, to mature, to expand, to become a person, as is his destiny.

DR. PAUL TOURNIER

CONTENTS

Concerning the Necessity and Frequency of Conflict in Marriage

> "The problem of love belongs to the realm of human suffering. We need not be ashamed that everyone of us must pay his tribute in the coin of the realm."
>
> C. G. JUNG

It may seem strange that a book about happier marriages should begin with an affirmation of the necessity of conflict in marriage and that, in addition, it should stress the high frequency of such conflict from the outset. Many marriages would benefit greatly if husband and wife only knew that conflict in marriage is inevitable, that it belongs indeed to the essence of marriage. It is characteristic of human nature always to expect the best, the finest, the happiest of fates for ourselves. If we could only make up our minds to learn something from the experience of all of our fellowmen and be content to look for a happiness which is of this world and therefore less than perfect, we would eliminate many sources of bitter disappointment. Husband and wife could then give up holding each other guilty merely because their marriage did not result in untroubled, idyllic bliss. And that alone would be a net gain.

Marriage is something alive, and anything alive is bipolar; that is to say, it draws its life from the tensions between two poles. Such tensions result in shocks, always and everywhere, and marriage is no exception. Physicians, psychologists, judges, clergymen, and even experienced married people all agree that nowadays there are hardly any marriages without occasional tensions, indeed without occasional severe crises. This does not suggest that we are today less well prepared for marriage than we used to be. It is rather that our more pronounced differentiation, our heightened consciousness, makes it more difficult for us to negotiate the business of marriage, to subordinate ourselves to a common ideal. There are also certain trends which are hostile to marriage; for example, the notion that any marriage can be easily dissolved, the crowding of people into cities, or the absence of tradition in contemporary society. All these trends naturally increase the difficulties which await marriage. It is an encouraging sign that both the general public and specific individuals are increasingly becoming aware of these difficulties and seeking means to overcome them. Thus while marriage seems to be falling apart, the interest in the constantly growing number of books about marriage and the lively attendance at lectures on marriage offer evidence of an opposite trend which is good and sound and which, hopefully, points in the direction of the gradual recovery of modern marriage.

All marital difficulties can be traced to either external or internal causes, and we are all inclined to look for the causes of our troubles, not only in marriage but wherever we meet them, first of all in the external world. These external causes are, as a rule, much handier. Not only do they strike us more forcefully but they permit us to fix the blame for any clash or failure outside of ourselves. At this point, my experiences as a marriage counselor are in complete agreement with the experience of others engaged in counseling: it is much easier to recognize and to eliminate such external causes of difficulties as, for example, poor living conditions, financial straits, or trouble with the neighbors, than it is to uncover and to overcome the internal causes of marital conflicts.

Here it is much more difficult to see clearly. Therefore it is important that we discuss first of all these internal causes which can—and from time to time indeed must—lead to conflict and tensions in every marriage.

It is reasonable to compare marriage conflicts to physical illness, to conceive of them as breakdowns of the marital organism. Such an approach to conflict in marriage has much to commend it. The approach becomes even more fruitful when we apply to the phenomenon of conflict in marriage an insight which modern medicine has been applying increasingly to many ills of the body, namely, that they are actually efforts on the part of nature to expel whatever substances are causing the sickness.

According to this concept, conflict in marriage is not something accidental, something which merely happens to the marital organism. It is rather an attempt of the living marital organism to achieve its objective, a truly harmonious union, by neutralizing or overcoming whatever disturbing influences may be emanating from one partner or the other. When crises in marriage are so understood and so accepted by the partners, they become stages in a meaningful development of the marriage community rather than a meaningless sequence of isolated disturbances. No longer does the unhappy wife or the man disappointed in his marriage get bogged down in the question, "Why do I have to suffer so in my marriage?"—a question which frequently and all too readily assumes a far more dangerous form, namely, "Who is responsible for my unhappiness in this marriage?" The answer which we are likely to give in silence and, more often, in loud arguments, usually points a finger at the attitude of our partner rather than at our own attitude. And many marriage partners have found to their own great harm that this line of marital argument leads straight into a dead end.

But if both partners understand that it is advisable —in illness or marital counseling or indeed any of the manifestations of life—to explore not just the causes but the meaning, they will ask themselves: "Where is the present tension leading us? *To what end* are we experiencing these disappointments, this pain?" Such a question is oriented to the *future.* The answer to this question is far more likely to yield clues for a constructive and positive attitude, whereas the "Why?" question is arrested in the past and necessarily implies judgment or even condemnation. The "Why?" question produces guilty parties, the

"To what end?" question, hopeful ones. Of course, it would be irresponsible to hope for a happier future for the marriage if the causes which produced the crisis were not also resolutely eliminated. But any internal transformation receives a victorious impetus only when it is animated by a discovery of meaning which points to the future.

Of course, just as a man can perish from a bodily ailment, even so a marriage can perish as a result of conflict escalated into crisis. Whether a crisis leads to healing or to destruction depends in large part upon the marriage partners. The Greek physician Hippocrates once said: "All sickness is both divine and human." One might say the same thing about crisis in marriage. Much would be gained if the partners could admit that such conflicts are not likely to be grounded exclusively in the human imperfection of the spouse but that something of a healing nature may be hidden in them which may be well worth exploring. Our subsequent discussion is designed to lay some groundwork for such an insight.

The Two Fundamental Psychic Attitudes

"In love, we usually pledge ourselves to a celestial being only to find that we are pledged to a being of this earth."

CHARLES TSCHOPP

The internal causes of conflict which we have been discussing are bound up with the very essence of marriage or at least with the essence of the marriage partners. They are not the result of the particularly blameworthy conduct of one spouse or the other. Rather they are present from the very moment at which the marriage, the intimate and lasting sharing of the life of two distinct persons, begins.

Extensive investigations of married couples have revealed that at least 70% of all marriages are so-called marriages of contrast, that is, marriages in which the partners markedly differ in a number of respects, both physical and psychological.

The particular investigation to which we are referring was carried out by Kretschmer, a psychiatrist and student of the human constitution, who began with a study of the bodily frame of the mates. It soon appeared that body build was closely paralleled by certain fundamental psychic attitudes. According to Kretschmer, there are two basic forms of the human frame—the pyknic and the leptosome.

Pyknic man is likely to be thick-set, rotund, with large body cavities (head, chest, abdomen). Leptosome man is likely rather to be thin-set. He may be tall or short, and is marked chiefly by his slenderness.

Far more important for our subject is the fact that there are distinct psychological differences which correspond to these bodily differences. Pyknic man is, in most cases, *extroverted, turned outward.* Leptosome man, thin-set, is most frequently *introverted, turned inward.*

These two important concepts can be more clearly grasped by answering the following questions. Whoever can respond with a rapid, unhesitating *yes* to the first three questions is likely to be predominantly extroverted. Whoever responds to the three subsequent questions with a *yes* is likely to be predominantly introverted. Obviously there are all kinds of shadings between these two fundamental psychic attitudes, but for clarity's sake, we shall not deal with any of them.

The first three questions are:

"Do you gladly invite people you have not met before?"

"Do you have many friends?"

"Do you find it easy to forgive?"

The other three questions are:

"Do you stick pretty close to rules and habits?"

"Are you reserved?"

"Are you disturbed when you receive a letter with a mutilated address?"

Most people decide rather readily for one or the other of these two groups. However, for the sake of what follows, it will be necessary for us to describe the personality of extrovert and introvert in greater detail. In so doing, let us bear in mind, as has been noted, that in most marriages one of the spouses is primarily extroverted, the other primarily introverted. Thus we will readily suspect, even on the basis of a rather incomplete description, that the partners will, indeed will have to, react very differently in many situations. And it follows, of course, that in a number of cases tension and conflict will arise.

It is a basic trait of the extrovert, the person turned outward, constantly to be spending himself. He enters deeply into every experience. He virtually loses himself in life. The fundamental attitude of the introvert, the person turned inward, consists rather in defending himself against outside claims. His concern is to secure for himself a position of maximum security and power. Picturesquely speaking, it may be possible to compare the extrovert to water which always adapts itself to outward forms, running and tumbling in whatever direction it is able to flow, forever losing its own form and taking on the shape of its surroundings. Thus, while the extrovert believes that he is conquering his environment, the conquest may be highly compulsive. By contrast, the introvert may be likened to a block of granite. He possesses a firm, fixed form which he tries to imprint, if the occasion arises, upon his environment, for example, upon the water which surrounds him or the earth on which he rests. He does not know that he is doing this. He certainly does not "will" it. But he is doing it just the same. Just ask the extroverted partner!

The extrovert lives above all in his relationships with

the world, in his exchange with his fellowmen. He acts upon and spontaneously affirms the world. The introvert is more likely to shut himself off from the outside world. For him it is the inner world that counts. He does not adapt himself to the world: he rather expects the world to adapt itself to him, that is, to his principles and rules. The introvert thus possesses a certain inner solidity, definiteness, consistency, even though these qualities occasionally escalate into rigidity. By contrast, the extrovert often lacks such a secure grasp. He risks losing himself in the outer world. He adapts himself to it and cannot help being engaged in constant commerce with it, even though this commerce is not necessarily of a friendly nature. The distance which the introvert maintains between himself and others stands in stark contrast to this close involvement of the extrovert with the world. While the extrovert stands in danger of losing himself to the world, the introvert is threatened by a lonely fate. He cannot get out of himself and is often imprisoned by his own reserve. Whenever life threatens to take hold of the introvert, to sweep him along, he instinctively defends himself. He wants to remain in control. He will not become an object of life but insists on remaining a self-determining subject. This tendency to hold on to himself is also the hallmark of that self-love which comes to the fore when a man prizes his own unchangeability more than his community with the marriage partner. And the introvert often cherishes his unchangeability with unusual tenacity, even though this is the very characteristic he will have to sacrifice, sooner or later, if he wants to find the way to his mate, if he wants really to love. For to love means, for the introvert, to outgrow himself. The extrovert, on the other hand, will have to find himself in the experience of love. He will have to overcome his fickleness and lack of direction by faithfulness and constancy. The introvert wants everything or nothing. The extrovert says, "Live and let live."

The introvert, however, is by no means without feeling, even though he may occasionally appear that way to the extrovert. His feelings are merely restrained and therefore less apparent. Kretschmer describes the psyche of the introvert graphically as a Roman villa which, with its closed shutters, appears cool and lifeless on the outside, while inside a party is going on. The extrovert, on the other hand, is characterized by his apparently excellent, though often superficial, contact with all kinds of people—on the train, on the streetcar, at the stadium. He has a great need for companionship. The introvert does not have nearly as much need for contact; in fact, his capacity for contact is far less. He is capable of genuine friendship, but his friends are likely to be a small select group. He avoids becoming involved with just anybody.

The introvert insists upon choosing his surroundings rather than simply accepting any environment and company—which the extrovert does so naturally. The introvert feels best in an atmosphere of reserve, calm, coolness. He prefers a world in which people don't live too close to each other so that it is not necessary always to collide with one's fellowman. The introvert makes his way with the least effort in aristocratic society, or in the mechanized, predictable operation of office or factory, or again in the solitude and beauty of nature. Occasionally he will temper his loneliness by acquiring a pet. People who attach themselves more closely to pets than to fellow humans are most likely to be introverts. Pets are faithful and selfless companions who do not pry into our secrets and from whom we need not hide anything. In their presence, the introvert can freely give himself without revealing himself and his innermost being which he simply cannot do in the presence of "strangers." In the presence of people, the introvert performs differently, insofar as he does not feel close to them. He feels the need constantly to protect his feelings from their intrusions.

Polite speech is the method used at all levels of society to secure such protection. Through the conventions of polite speech, we maintain contact with our environment in an impersonal but nevertheless cultivated and generally accepted way, without being compelled to expose our personal and private feelings, mood, and thoughts. For the extrovert, the forms of polite speech are rather an obstacle, a brake imposed on him by society, which prevents him from expressing himself with entire spontaneity in his lively relations with the outside world. On the other hand, his training in politeness and social conventions protects the extrovert from making his feelings of attraction or dislike toward others unacceptably explicit. For if he let himself go, he would be in trouble most of the time!

The characterization of these two basic types has been necessarily much too schematic. However, we can see quite clearly what a wide range of different reactions can be expected from these types. And we must insist again that we are dealing with differences which belong to the very essence of these two types. Each thus must, by his very nature, exhibit the general attitudes and reaction patterns which we have been sketching. Each does so with a clear conscience, indeed with the conviction that he would be untrue to his essence were he to act otherwise.

Let us illustrate these differences in attitudes and the possibilities for conflict which may result from them by means of two short scenes from the ordinary experience of a married couple.

Husband and wife are going downtown on a shopping trip. The woman, an introvert, has a fairly specific plan; in any case she knows exactly what she wants to buy. She has a clear inner picture of what she is looking for. Shopping, for her, means to seek and acquire the object which corresponds as closely as possible to this picture. The man, an extrovert, is oriented altogether differently. He has only a vague image of what he wants to buy, and is not at all certain about such matters as price range or quality or the precise appearance of the object in view. He will enter the store prepared to explain rather long-windedly what he is looking for, willing in advance to be counseled and convinced. He will select something from what he is being shown, and he may not even notice that he has allowed himself to be sold something which corresponds only in the most general way to his original intention. His introverted wife, on the other hand, explains clearly and precisely what she wants, so that the saleslady knows exactly what to show her. And if she is shown anything other than the desired object, she will make it unmistakably clear that this does not fit, this is too large, this is too expensive or the wrong color, etc. For the introvert, the whole transaction will take place in an atmosphere of cool objectivity, while the extrovert may be carried away to indulge in personal comments or be drawn into conversation about things which have more to do with his relating to the human environment than with the purchase itself.

How then will this husband and this wife react to their respective performances in the store? If they happen to be in a phase of mutual understanding and harmony, each is likely to accept the different behavior of the other calmly and without taking offense. But suppose that their relationship is aggravated by some prior difference of opinion. In that case, the introverted wife will experience the long-windedness of her extroverted husband as painful. She will think that he never knows what he wants, that he is causing needless work for the saleslady, and that in the end he will allow himself to be sold a bill of goods.

The extroverted husband, on the other hand, indulges in a similar judgment, quiet or vocal, upon the conduct of his introverted wife in the store. He finds his wife far too critical in all purchases. He feels that she holds on to what she has had in mind far too rigidly. Perhaps he throws her rigidity in her face. She is an unattractive customer, she does not accept good advice, and she is generally haughty and cool toward people and does not treat them as persons but as numbers. The wife replies that her husband engages in unnecessary personal discussions with salespeople, which is something he finds entirely natural and right because of his spontaneous need for contact.

The reproaches which this husband and his wife are making to each other are both ill-founded and well-founded. They are well-founded because they reflect precisely the impression which each has of the other, or, more precisely, of the *appearance* of the other. They are ill-founded and therefore wounding because they misjudge the *essence* of the reproached spouse. We shall return to this point later.

Let us now observe another couple who, by some accident, have landed in the middle of a very loud party. This time let the man be the introverted type and the woman the extrovert. What will happen here? The extroverted wife will soon be feeling very much at home in this company. She will participate, laugh with the rest, have a good time. She will rejoice in the fact that for once she happens to find herself in less proper surroundings. By contrast, the introverted husband is not enjoying himself at all in this situation. Even though nothing offensive is being said or done, he is nonetheless painfully affected by the boisterousness of the company. In his opinion, all the guests are letting themselves go a bit too much and are not showing sufficient reserve. He will be sitting on the sidelines, as it were. He will probably try not to be rude, but eventually he will remind his wife that it is time to leave—too early in her eyes—and his good-bye to the company will be rather abrupt, even though mannerly.

On the way home, then, the extroverted wife is likely to reproach her husband for being a spoilsport, unable to adapt himself, possessed by a superiority complex, and unsociable: in short, he has conducted himself impossibly once again.

"But I've been thinking the very same thing about you," replies the introverted husband. "You simply have no manners. You don't know what is proper. You observe no limits whatever. I call such conduct lacking in dignity. In my opinion, a woman should have standards. She should be aware of the boundaries of correct behavior."

Thus both believe that their judgment is correct, and each feels wounded by the judgment of the other. The husband thinks that his wife has simply no understanding for his innermost being, and vice versa. The extroverted wife finds her husband insufferably proper and boring. He, in his turn, is probably sighing over the fact that the upbringing of the children has to be entrusted to a woman who is so little aware of what is proper and who sets such an imperfect example for the children.

Nevertheless, these two persons are in all likelihood profoundly loyal to each other. The introverted husband, when the times are good, loves the spontaneous, warmly alive being of his wife, whereas she feels guarded and protected by his firm, calm, reserved way. In fact, she was able to let herself go at that party in such a free and carefree manner and to have such a good time precisely because she was aware of him at her side. And for this she is grateful to him, even if for the moment her anger at his reserve at the party has the upper hand.

With this last remark, we are calling attention to something peculiar which up to now has been largely neglected in the study of psychology. We have in mind the fact that a married person does not react the same way, does not conduct himself in the same way, in the marriage as outside the marriage, and that this is not just a matter of convention or upbringing. It seems that, since in any working marriage we are closely connected with another person, this fact itself often automatically releases certain psychological tendencies while inhibiting others. Thus the psychology of marriage is not just the psychology of two individuals. Its hitherto largely unrealized autonomy is grounded in the condition in which two closely connected and mutually complementary partners are able to discover new opportunities and find new tasks. In this sense each partner should try, if only for his own benefit, to outgrow himself and to become a part of the new organism, of a mutually complementary married *couple* whose members stand in contrast one to the other, yet pursue a true union. The concept of "couple" deserves a great deal more attention in the psychology of marriage. In the first place, it points to the fact that the mates must be attuned to each other in a quite specific way, else they are not suited for each other. In the second place, the concept of "couple" expresses the fact that, if the two persons have actually become a mutually complementary entity, this entity is something more than the sum total of the two persons. As members of a couple, they are offered fresh possibilities while taking on new duties and tasks.

Complementation Through Difference

"The meeting of two personalities is like the mixing of two different substances. Inasmuch as they mix at all, they are both changed."

C. G. JUNG

In his depth, every man harbors a strong, irresistible need for complementation, for fulfillment. This need is portrayed in many ancient myths, most emphatically in the Greek myth according to which the soul of every man is embarked on a longing search for a sister soul with whom he was once united in a blissful union, before history began.

As a result of this inborn need for "the other half," the extrovert looks precisely for the introvert who is so different and therefore able to complement his being, and vice versa. This need, deeply grounded in the essence of life and of the soul, is probably the reason why the choice of a mate so frequently leads to a complementary combination. The more extreme extrovert a man is, the more markedly he tends to seek out an extremely introverted woman for his partner. It seems as if nature were using this complementation drive to eliminate the extremes so that, by the mingling of extremes, the human species might ever continue down the middle of the road.

Thus it may be that the individual is entrusted with a task, for the sake of maintaining the species, which taxes his psychic capacity to the utmost. However, this task also happens to be in his personal interest in that it fosters his own unique development and maturation.

The essential difference between the extrovert and the introvert cannot fail to cause many differences of opinion and many tensions. The extrovert likes to go out, to bring friends to the house, to participate in noisy and usually unorganized activities. The introvert prefers to be alone or, at least, in well-behaved, carefully chosen company. To the extrovert, the introverted partner appears unduly cold, offensively reserved, immovable, unwilling to entertain all kinds of whims and moods. The introvert, in his turn, is offended by the lack of order, and, frequently, the tactlessness, of the extrovert who will not restrain his feelings and opinions. The introvert is likely to reproach the extrovert for being oriented almost exclusively to the immediate moment. The extrovert will reproach the introvert for clinging to rules, habits, and customs, for forcing life into prescriptions and thus spoiling it. Thus the partners seem to be at odds with each other in just about all respects.

But the more deeply the partners are able to fathom the difference between the respective orientations, the better they will be able to understand that they are dealing with fundamental attitudes that cannot be given up or even materially changed. The sooner, too, will they be able to understand that their divergent attitudes rest upon a foundation conditioned by nature itself. Thus they will not be as likely to suspect each other of ill will, obtuseness, or bad manners, but will come to regard and to accept each other's differences as given by nature. In this way, the basic difference between husband and wife loses much of its conflict potential. It can now be accepted much like a natural phenomenon which may not be pleasant, which cannot be changed either by scolding or by taking offense. Are we not used to taking rain in our stride as something we cannot change? When it rains, we stay at home or else we take a raincoat and an umbrella for our protection. We do not attempt to change the rain; we try to adapt ourselves to it. This is precisely the process of transformation which the partners in this marriage must attempt with respect to their respective differences. By this process, much severe conflict can be prevented in the marriage. Just as we may be able to find beauty in the rain and to enjoy it, even so the different nature of a husband or wife may suddenly appear in a new light as a result of such a neutral and objective attitude. No longer will the difference irritate us. Rather, we will find it delightful!

There is one thing, however, which the partners who possess such different fundamental attitudes must always keep in view: it is not possible for either one of them to ascertain the essence of the other, only its manifestation. Conversely, each knows his own essence but not its manifestations; that is to say, he is unable to give a precise account of how his essence appears to the other, how he affects the other.

Judging the other on the basis of mere appearance understandably invites injustice to the essence of the other. When times are good, the other is idealized. In times of marital disharmony, he is greatly depreciated. Always there is danger of misunderstanding, as long as it is not possible to understand the essence of the other from within. And it matters little whether this misunderstanding ignores reality with a positive or a negative bias: the result is undesirable in any case. On the one hand, disillusionment is bound to follow sooner or later. On the other hand, it is deeply wounding to be misunderstood and depreciated by the person closest to us.

As soon as the partners understand and accept their respective natures, an inner harmony emerges which can furnish an extremely useful basis for a genuine rather than merely apparent understanding. In our naïveté, we always tend to assume that our partner possesses the same opinions, the same reaction patterns and inclinations as we do. This tendency is more marked for the introvert than it is for the extrovert. And while the difference between the spouses may be insignificant and unnoticeable in all particulars, it is nonetheless fated to lead to deep and unbridgeable opposition because it is an essential difference. Disagreements over particular matters will then be all the more disturbing, if the couple fails to realize that they are dealing with a decisive difference in perception which may seem small but which really is the cause of the tension. The major error is to try to resolve the difference in its own terms, by placing the blame on the judgment of the mate, whereas the difference is actually the result of the application of the different yardsticks: it is a matter of divergent mental attitudes.

The Two
Pairs of Types

Careful observation of numerous married couples has proved that the striving for complementation, which we have been discussing, has some specific and significant effects upon the choice of a mate and thus upon behavior in marriage and marital difficulties. At this point I have something to say which, to my knowledge, has not been noted anywhere, at least in this form, in the literature of marriage, but which, on the basis of my practical experience as marriage counselor, has a great deal to contribute toward the understanding and the relief of marital difficulties and tensions.

It is possible to divide people, according to their fundamental psychic attitudes, not only into extroverts and introverts but also into four large subgroups. It is characteristic of these subgroups that members of any subgroup explore the world and react to the world with a different instrument—with a different "function." I am talking about the so-called *functional types* first described by C. G. Jung.[1]

There are people who approach the world primarily through the medium of thought. Their actions depend above all on their thinking. They judge everything pri-

---

[1]C. G. Jung, *Psychological Types* (New York: Pantheon Books Inc., 1959). See also the excellent description of these types and the elaboration, from a medical-psychological point of view, of many related problems by J. H. van der Hoop, *Types of Consciousness* (Bern: Hans Huber).

marily in terms of true or false. Jung calls these people
thinking types. The thinking type is complemented by
the so-called feeling type. The feeling type is determined
predominantly by his emotions. He judges things mainly
in terms of good or bad, perhaps in terms of attractive or
unattractive. These two types are located, according to
Jung, along the same axis, the so-called rational, or
measuring, axis because they measure or judge all things,
whether by means of thought or by means of emotion.
(See diagram.)

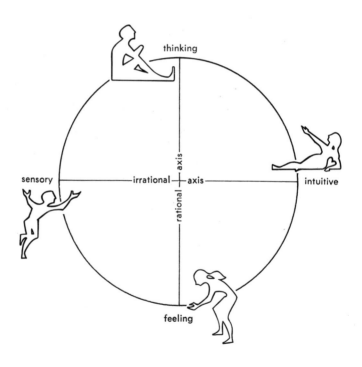

There is also a second pair of types which may be characterized by the opposite poles marked intuitive and sensory. The intuitive type perceives the world mainly through a kind of inner eye. Whenever he finds himself in a given situation or face to face with a particular person, he discovers within himself a quite definite attitude which has taken hold of him with great certainty and which will guide his action and reactions. This attitude is based not so much on certain external factors as on a kind of inner experience. The opposite type described as sensory or instinctive perceives the world much more from the outside, from the surface. He lives by the senses and may also be designated as sensual. He lives in terms of color, smell, temperature, sun, light, beauty, movement, in short, all things concrete and palpable. The intuitive type on the other hand is captivated not by the senses but by the "sense," the meaning of things. Therefore he has a particular appreciation for symbols, for meaning connections, for the possibilities of any situation. In contrast with the first pair of types, the measuring or judging pair, these types do not judge. They merely note, describe, ascertain. Unlike the thinking and the feeling types, they do not possess any precise order of moral values. This does not mean, however, that they are immoral. Intuitive people in particular are likely to have a lively religious feeling or, generally speaking, an inner assurance of their dependence upon something greater, something of a cosmic nature. But both the sensory type and the intuitive type approach the world and people with a certain detachment which may be heightened to fickleness, the same detachment which can

be found in amoral persons. Their ability to adapt themselves to any circumstances, to accept life as it is, to enjoy
it or at least make the best of it, arouses the indignation
or, sometimes, the envying admiration of the rational,
that is, valuing types. They call this detachment lack of
character or crass opportunism, or else independence and
adaptability. For the rational types, principles and order
are far more significant and real than they are for the
irrational types who are so strongly oriented toward what
is given, what actually exists. (Let us not be confused by
the terms "rational" and "irrational" which C. G. Jung
uses in a rather unusual way. A. von Orelli has proposed
for the two pairs of types the designations "egotrop,"
aimed at the ego, and "cosmotrop," aimed at the world.
For thinking and emotion participate decisively in the
upbuilding of the ego, whereas intuition and sensation
relate the ego to the world.)

The rational types, that is, the feeling and thinking
types, tend to feel a heavy responsibility for what goes
on in the world around them. They are inclined to ascribe
a significant role to the will, their own or that of others,
in whatever transpires. This is no doubt related to the
fact that they see the world mainly from the standpoint
of their system of values to which they refer everything.
When something agrees with their system of values, they
describe it as right (thinking type) or good (feeling
type). When something contradicts their system of
values, it is false or bad. Events or things which have no
direct bearing upon their system of values will be ignored
by these types as unimportant or accidental.

The much more world-oriented cosmotropes or irrational types do not make any judgmental selection among the events and things of which they take note and by which they allow themselves to be determined. They are far more aware of what the other types regard as "accidental," that is to say, incomprehensible, ill-fitting, or unwanted, and therefore they are less prone to make themselves or others responsible for the course of events.

This obviously highly schematic description of the two pairs of types has seemed desirable, because experience shows that marriage partners belong, in the overwhelming majority of cases, to the same pair of types or, to put it in terms of the above diagram, to the same axis. In other words, both partners are as a rule either rational or irrational types.

Upon closer scrutiny, it appears in addition that in a rational pair, one of the partners, usually the man, belongs to the thinking pole whereas the other partner, usually the woman, to the feeling pole. A thinking man is thus frequently married to a feeling woman. In our scheme, therefore, the two marriage partners appear most of the time *at opposite poles.*

The same holds true for the other, the irrational pair of types. In such couples, one of the partners is ordinarily a sensory type, the other an intuitive type. Here, however, classification becomes more complicated. For one thing, there is no such clear predominance of one sex or the other at either pole as there is on the rational axis. Women are more frequently sensory types than intuitive ones and men are intuitive types more frequently than sensory ones, but the reverse constellation also occurs rather frequently. In the second place, sensory types often do not know whether perchance they are intuitive types, and vice versa. This may be the result of the low degree of consciousness in these types. However, similar doubts hardly ever occur on the rational axis. A thinking type will hardly ever mistake himself for a feeling type, nor a feeling type for a thinking type, except for some rather unusual cases of masculine feeling types and feminine thinking types.

If we now proceed to relate our earlier discussion of the relationship between extroverts and introverts to what we have just set forth about the two pairs of types, we arrive at the conclusion that to each type there corresponds a fairly definite partner. *The partner of an introvert will be an extrovert. Both will be placed on the same axis but usually at opposite poles.* Thus the couples we are most likely to observe in life present the following combinations.

Rational axis:
Extroverted thinking type—introverted feeling type.
Introverted thinking type—extroverted feeling type.
Irrational axis:
Extroverted intuitive type—introverted sensory type.
Introverted intuitive type—extroverted sensory type.

Of course this sounds highly schematic, and it must be understood that the schema represents a gross oversimplification of the complexity of life. On the other hand, neither these combinations nor the types which they involve have been dreamed up in someone's study. Daily observation has demonstrated their reality and the frequency of their occurrence.

Here we stumble into a peculiar analogy with one of

the decisive discoveries of modern chemistry. It used to be assumed that any chemical substance could combine in just about any way with any other chemical substance. Upon closer investigation, however, it was discovered that in reality this was by no means the case. Rather, certain combinations occur far more frequently than others. On the basis of this observation, it then became possible to bring some order into the apparently senseless multiplicity of combinations and, according to certain points of view, to discover some regularities. Something similar in principle is opened up for the psychology of marriage by the application of Jung's functional types. It may become possible, someday, to sort out, from the multiplicity of disturbances in marriage, the difficulties and developments characteristic of particular constellations of types. Not only marriage counseling but even behavior in marriage might as a result be easier to learn, so that young married people might occasionally be spared learning their lesson at their own expense.

It goes without saying, however, that the complexity of life can never be comprehended in such a schema. In the first place, the types themselves are the result of severe abstraction and therefore less than true to life. They naturally neglect what is unique to any man in favor of what is general and typical. In the second place, every one of these types has a number of subtypes which arise in consideration of the so-called "auxiliary functions" which we shall discuss briefly later. In the third place, any typological classification of an individual inevitably deals with only a part of his being and neglects a multitude of decisively important factors. In spite of these significant limitations however, this typology has proved itself so useful and handy both in marriage counseling and in the marriage relationship that it seems desirable to describe in somewhat greater detail the particular types as well as the difficulties and misunderstandings which attend particular combinations of types with almost uncanny regularity.

The fact that, in the use of this typology, the unique and the personal are being neglected in favor of the typical and the general, proves to be highly advantageous from a therapeutic point of view. This was, after all, a step which had to be taken in medicine when it became necessary to abstract what was recurrent and general from the uniqueness of the particular patient in order gradually to arrive at the delineation of particular sickness syndromes. Only in this way was it possible to transform an art which had been tied to the intuition of particular physicians into a science based upon intellectually communicable knowledge. Experience proves that something similar applies to the counseling of married people in search of help. Only as they achieve some distance from their personal needs and as they begin to discern the general and the typical behind the apparently unique crisis which threatens their person and their marriage will they find the necessary objectivity and, eventually, the indispensable power of love that will enable them to work things through to a new attitude. This new attitude will then make it possible for them to endure the weaknesses of the mate as part of the natural equipment of his psychological type rather than as the result of his particular and deliberate contrariness.

The Four
Functional Types

In discussing the thinking, feeling, sensory, and intuitive types, we will certainly not imply the thinking
type only thinks, the feeling type only feels, etc.

Every human being carries within himself all four
functions, just as every man possesses all the senses. But
just as it is possible to develop one of the five senses,
for example, the ear, or the eye, more prominently than
the rest, with the result that the other senses remain less
fully developed—just think of the highly developed sense
of touch of the blind—even so, in the psychological
realm, it appears that when a particular function is highly
developed, the function which, in the schema, occupies
the opposite pole, is usually poorly developed. This *undeveloped counter-function* will be discussed at some
length presently, because it happens to be the source of
many difficulties in marriage. In fact, this undeveloped
counter-function tends to be highly visible in any marriage disturbance. Frequently it is easier to identify the
correct type of a person on the basis of this undeveloped
function than on the basis of the highly developed one.
Thus, the presence of underdeveloped emotions makes it
probable that we are dealing with a thinking type. It is
often easier to recognize an intuitive type by the poor
performance of his sensory functions than by his intuition. The feeling type often gives himself away by his
lack of logic and his self-righteousness. The sensory type,
on the other hand, can often best be diagnosed by the

absence of whims and fancies, or, more likely, by the appearance of negative and undeveloped notions in the form of all sorts of worries about the future, etc. The description of the four types which follows will clarify all this.

The Thinking Type

In his study of types, C. G. Jung designates as thinking types all persons who perceive and try to regulate life primarily by means of thinking. In this type we find predominantly men. Pronounced thinking types are indeed rare among women. The typical feminine intelligence apparently makes use of other functions.

Thinking is based upon judgments that normally possess a certain general validity. To some extent, thinking can be learned. It is independent of time and place and consistent in its reasoning. Thus it becomes possible to construct entire systems through thinking. Such systems play a decisive role in the life of the thinking type. The questions "Why?" and "What for?" which thinking types quite often pose, whether consciously or unconsciously, belong to such a system—a system of causality and of finality. The fully developed thinking type characteristically uses clear concepts. He believes that he knows the exact grounds of his actions, and he expects the same of others. He is also inclined to assume that his wife operates in the same way, according to definite, logical, and generally valid laws, which is what he thinks he is doing. As a rule, this will not be so, since the wife of a thinking type is most likely to be a feeling type with a radically different orientation. The statement of August von Kotzebue is certainly correct: "Women carry their proofs in their hearts, men in their heads." But the pure thinking type does not tolerate such proofs of the heart. Therefore, the conduct of his wife frequently baffles him. And if her conduct doesn't suit him, he deprecatingly calls it "moody" or else he talks about "feminine logic."

To the thinking type, who as such is likely to possess an undeveloped feeling function, all emotion appears suspect. His thinking may well be indispensable in the practice of his profession, but the rigidity which is connected with it is likely to create a sober and soulless attitude toward his wife and children and thus restrain their spontaneity. His wife suffers from his lack of imagination and spiritual empathy. The husband, on the other hand, is very proud of his integrity and dependability and is willing to let it go at that, since such subtle things as feminine whims and moods, secret wishes, fads, and the like simply do not exist in his logical world. A thinking type in love, at least if he is an introvert, will feel very unsure toward women and will appear ridiculous to himself because of his awkward, underdeveloped emotions.

The undeveloped nature of the feeling function of the thinking type manifests itself also by his use of irony. When he is asked a question, he is likely to answer not good-naturedly but ironically, aggressively, pointedly. By using irony, the thinking type hides his feelings because he is dimly aware of their immaturity. He ridicules his feelings, he depreciates them in advance, for fear his

mate will depreciate and abuse them. He does not dare
rely on his feelings completely, even though his emotions are likely to be, in such cases, rather tender and
sensitive even though unsure, vulnerable, and ill adapted
to life.

The moods of men are likely to be the undeveloped
shapes of rather massive emotions of, for example, dissatisfaction with the world or the employer or something
else. Moody men seldom understand why they are in a
bad mood. This very fact proves that our moods are
closely connected with undeveloped, unconscious functions of our psyche. The well-known, somewhat con-
descending tenderness of certain "regular customers"
toward waitresses may also be a symptom of their in-
ferior ability to express emotion.

Reactions which express feelings fully and truthfully
do not fit into the world of the thinking type. Therefore
he does not take them seriously; and his wife, herself
usually a feeling type, is distinctly and painfully aware of
this. She is likely to react to her husband's incompre-
hension with even more vehement emotions, which he,
in turn, understands even less and discounts as hysteria.
Eventually he says, "I don't understand my wife." What
he ought to say is, "I don't understand emotions."

The Feeling Type

Let us now turn to the feeling pole of the rational
axis, to the feeling type. While at the thinking pole we
encounter largely men, the feeling types are predomi-

nantly women. In examining the feeling function, it becomes quite clear that the extroverted and the introverted feeling types behave very differently in many respects, whereas with the thinking type, the differences between extrovert and introvert are far less marked. The extroverted thinking type is above all a practical person; the introverted thinking type is more theoretically inclined.

The extroverted feeling type is, by her very nature, oriented to her environment in terms of emotional rapport. She seeks such rapport constantly. She needs such rapport in order to feel well. Rapport with her fellowman is, for her, a vital necessity. Her feelings adapt themselves to the external world with reliable promptness. In gay company she is gay, and in sad company, sad. She just cannot help participating with animation and abandon. If she fails to create a positive, that is, a sympathetic, rapport with her surroundings, she will try at least to build a rapport by means of a good fight. It goes without saying that any woman who is so greatly dependent upon emotional participation in the outside world will be profoundly unhappy when she is not being understood by those closest to her. And who indeed is closer to such a feminine feeling type than her own husband and children? Whenever such a woman feels misunderstood, the whole world seems dark to her; life makes no sense. Conversely, she will be particularly joyful when she feels emotionally in tune with her surroundings.

As a rule, extroverted feeling types have many acquaintances. They are always ready to strike up new friendships. They find contacts everywhere. They are active, they enjoy singing, they say hello in all directions, they love children, and they know all their neighbors and their stories.

But just as the feelings of the thinking type are undeveloped, so the thinking function of the feeling type remains unconsciously undeveloped. Therefore, it is particularly difficult for such a woman to be objective and, above all, to discuss anything objectively. She pronounces definite opinions, usually grounded in emotional experiences, and from these opinions she will not be budged. If you try to prove the contrary to her by means of quiet and rational arguments she may hear you out, if you are lucky, but she will keep coming right back, endlessly, to her own opinion. It was no doubt in this context that Edward Moerike once remarked, "It is dreadful to fight with women!" And even Frederick Schiller, creator of many ideal feminine figures, has written: "Are you not like women, who constantly return to their first word, even after hour-long, reasonable discussion?"

Masculine logic is of no help here. Feeling types often disguise their opinions as religious truths. Or else they try to buttress their point of view with reference to a biblical passage or some other authority—the family doctor, a neighbor lady, anyone. They are simply not accessible to reasoned debate. And when they run out of arguments, they are likely to conclude, "Men are heartless!"

The introverted feeling type differs from the extroverted feeling type, which we have just described, on some important points. She is much harder to identify as a feeling type because she holds back her emotions so that they operate within her rather than emanate from her. The emotions of this type are very fully developed and finely shaded. While the extroverted feeling type is oriented above all to *contact*, it is *tact* which plays a dominant role for the introverted feeling type. Introverted feeling types have a particularly fine flair for what is appropriate in a given situation, what one does or does not do. They are, as it were, life's natural-born mistresses of ceremonies. This constitutes at the same time their chief strength and their special danger. They are guardians of convention. They know instinctively how to handle all forms of social intercourse. However, they also tend to get bogged down in mores and customs and find it hard to free themselves from them. The most important traits of the introverted feeling type are a high sense of duty and dependability. Frequently she also possesses a marked artistic bent. As a rule, she is friendly, but not cordial and warmhearted like the extroverted feeling type.

Introverted feeling types positively dread to reveal their feelings. They instantly withdraw into themselves when the slightest danger arises that their feelings might be misunderstood, let alone ridiculed. This retreat into themselves makes it extraordinarily difficult for those closest to them to understand them and to maintain contact with them.

Extroverted *thinking* types, a combination usually represented by men, will find it very hard to understand the refined, hypersensitive emotional reactions of this feminine type. He will therefore discount some of her reactions as incomprehensible, as just "moods," and will react to them with predictable distaste.

After a quarrel, introverted feeling types are strongly inclined to withdraw into themselves. If misunderstandings and tensions occur frequently, such a woman will lose her rapport with her husband more and more. Experience shows that she will seek the reasons for his failure to understand her, in the final analysis, within herself, and that she will often react with feelings of inferiority and guilt. In this condition, she will be very unhappy. It will seem to her as if life were passing her by. And if she continues to develop in this direction, she will soon present us with the prototype of the "misunderstood wife." If the husband wants to find a way to his wife in spite of all these difficulties, he will have to build up her sense of self first of all. To do so, he will have to be convinced of the survival of all the fine and tender qualities of his wife, now deeply buried under layers of bad temper, wounded feelings, and excessive sensitivity. He will have to search for these buried qualities with the unshakable faith of a treasure hunter. Such patient efforts of the husband may indeed awaken in the wife a sense of her own worth. "If my husband takes such pains with me, I still must be worth something to him; I apparently mean more to him than I thought I did." This is what she may conclude, much to her relief. In such an atmosphere, her inner security may gradually come to life again. She may be able once more to offer her best gifts and to stand beside her husband as wife and mother, with her reserved but finely shaded feelings.

What we have said about the undeveloped thinking function of the extroverted feeling type applies in similar fashion to the introverted feeling type except that collisions with the outside world, while perhaps less frequent, are likely to be the more violent and thus prone to upset the marriage relationship lastingly.

The above-mentioned special qualities of the introverted feeling type—her high sense of duty, dependability, flair for convention—are often the starting point for differences of opinion between such a woman and her entirely different husband, who is likely to be an extroverted thinking type. As an extrovert, he tends toward a certain lack of organization. As a thinking type, he is likely to undervalue feelings. He will be oriented far more toward actual conditions than toward fixed mores and customs. Therefore he is likely to appear to his introverted feeling type wife as unreliable, aimless, perhaps even unstable, and she will take him to task accordingly. The extroverted husband, in his turn, will at such times stress the rigid, immovable and to him incomprehensible, "moody" nature of his introverted feeling type wife. And this mutual judgment, in which each sees only the negative side of the other and forgets the positive, will strike both as unjust. True, such judgment is in a degree unjust, and the injustice naturally hampers mutual understanding severely.

The Sensory Type

We now proceed to a discussion of the second pair of types. Let us turn first to the sensory type. This type lives above all by what is concrete, palpable, visible. He is oriented chiefly to the practical value of all things.

Utility plays a big part in his sober world. Unlike the intuitive type, he does not like it when things are represented or handled in a complicated way. This confuses him. For a sensory type to be feeling well, the situation into which he enters must be neither too strange nor too new. His reactions have something instinctive about them and are therefore tied to certain simple and so to speak preconceived schemes. The sensory type is often rather conservative, which does not prevent him, however, from being at the same time pretty capricious. His behavior has a strongly reactive character: left to his own devices, he is rather lame and cheerless. But when he is set to a specific task which suits him well, he is suddenly filled with life and activity and is able to react energetically and to assert himself effectively.

The sensory type is therefore dependent upon his mate for activation, at least to a certain extent, insofar as his mate can entrust him with a task which corresponds to his nature, that is, a useful task, one that produces money or recognition. Principles are of little significance for the sensory type, least of all if he is an extrovert. He feels no need for ordering his experiences systematically. Nevertheless, he frequently depends upon a certain tradition which to him represents a kind of self-defense, lest he lose himself altogether.

Among sensory types, we find also the hedonist for whom everything that affects the senses is of extraordinary importance. The hedonist can enjoy himself without making judgments and without a bad conscience. He can readily make his peace with the injustice which exists in the world, as long as it does not interfere with his capacity for pleasure. For many sensory types, the aesthetic has particular significance. They are experts at dressing tastefully and at beautifying their environment. The sensory type is likely to have a great flair for sports, dancing, movement, in short, everything that has to do with bodily sensations. His ideals are directed at a certain outward well-being and order: at house and yard, nice clothes, and often the arts.

The undeveloped counter-function of the sensory type is intuition. This absence of intuition manifests itself in his inability to perceive and experience actual, genuine, meaning connections. Instead of being a believer, he is readily inclined to superstition. The most zealous readers of horoscopes are found in this type. The sensory man will often have an intuitive woman as mate and will then regard her as an enthusiast or a dreamer. He will also reproach her for undue credulity and will have little patience for her neglect of appearances. In the sensory type, undeveloped intuition comes to the fore in his attitude toward the future. The sensory type frequently does not see any further possibilities, when for the intuitive type they are ever present. The sensory type is therefore likely to be anxious about the future: he torments himself with all sorts of worries about tomorrow. The introverted sensory type, for example, is likely to worry a great deal when he does not know the guests whom he is expecting. He worries about how he will greet them, what there will be to talk about, how he will conduct himself. All these very practical and concrete questions concerning the future bother the sensory type, making him anxious and fainthearted, while his intuitive mate is utterly uncomprehending, since for her these problems do not even exist.

The Intuitive Type

The orientation of the intuitive type differs radically from that of his most frequent partner, the sensory type. He sees things and people in a sense from within. For him, the world consists largely of relationships and possibilities for which he has a good flair. By the same token, he is likely to neglect what is palpable and near at hand. The intuitive type does not like to be tied down by promises and arrangements which he considers too rigid. He always wants to reserve some room for his inspirations, ideas, and impulses. These often take him by surprise: the extroverted intuitive type is particularly prone to them. Thus he has trouble observing rules and agreements: it is not possible to depend on him altogether. He has more impulsive energy than will power and perseverance. He stimulates action but is ordinarily short of "stick-to-itiveness." The intuitive type has a special talent for somehow escaping from all difficulties and for glossing over his mistakes.

With the intuitive type, it is the sensory function that is undeveloped. He tends to neglect or else to overrate anything that has to do with the senses—anything physical, concrete, time-bound. This comes to light, among other things, in the intuitive type's attitude toward his body. He is inclined either to neglect his bodily needs or else to attach undue significance to them.

Neglect of his body may take the form of a certain fool-hardiness. On the other hand, if he overrates his body he is likely to observe unrealistic and exaggerated dietary and hygienic measures which, for him, may become a lifefilling system, indeed a kind of substitute religion. The excessive worry of certain men about their health—their constant complaining, their tendency to become immersed in ailments for which women tend to make fun of them—is also related to their undeveloped sensory function.

Experience shows that intuitive types often develop relatively late in life, insofar as they do not respond as much to the growth-fostering stimuli of the outside world as do, for example, sensory types. Thus intuitive types frequently retain, for a rather long time, something childlike, radiant, innocent, naive; whereas sensory types awaken early and enter life's fray self-consciously and actively.

Intuitive types often have a poorly developed sense of money and of time. The intuitive type is either a spendthrift or a miser, not because he particularly values money but rather because he has no realistic appreciation of money. The same goes for his sense of time. He is always late, often misses the train, but nevertheless manages to reach his goal most of the time, thanks to his resourcefulness which enables him always to get help.

It goes without saying that this pattern of behavior is incomprehensible to the intuitive type's most frequent mate—to the punctual, alert, practical sensory type—and that we have here the source of many misunderstandings and clashes. The intuitive type, on the other hand, will have a hard time understanding the sensory type's anxious and uncertain orientation toward the future. For him, it is burdensome and unpleasant always to think through and to decide everything in advance, just to please his partner. The intuitive type resents being tied down to specific plans for a forthcoming vacation, the hour for coming home from some occasion, the use of certain monies. In all such commitments, the intuitive type sees shackles which coerce him to renounce subsequent, perhaps unexpected, possibilities. He lives most intensely when he stands on the threshold of a new situation. Thus to surrender in advance some of the possibilities of such a situation amounts, for him, to giving up some of the possibilities of life itself.

The sensory type often demands some renunciation of his partner, because, true to his nature, he prefers to choose the sure route. His generally anxious attitude toward the future, which he cannot clearly and concretely foresee, causes him either to avoid the hazards of uncertainty or, as far as possible, to insure himself against them. Thus he welcomes health insurance, life insurance, and all such security measures as necessary means for reassuring him about the future. The intuitive type, who does not worry about the future, exhibits a very different attitude toward these institutions. He seeks uncertainty and risk. The future does not daunt him. He is confident, perhaps overconfident, and therefore often fails to make even the simplest, most obvious provisions for the future.

When two persons of such different points of view engage in a common enterprise—for example, concern-

ing the future of the children, the expenditure of in-
come, or similar decisive questions—the difficulties which
are bound to arise in their marriage are so obvious that
we need not dwell on them to any extent.

A particular and very frequent burden upon the
marriage of this pair of types arises from the fact that
the sensory type comes to life, to clear self-consciousness,
rather early whereas the intuitive type gets there rather
late in life. The difficulty will be particularly severe when
the man happens to be the intuitive type, that is to say,
the mate who develops later. At the beginning of the
marriage, such a man is likely to be unable to provide
complete, masculine partnership for his alert and effective wife. It will be impossible for his wife, who is a
sensory type and therefore much in need of security, to
feel secure with him; and she will suffer greatly, and
often reluctantly, from the uncertainty in which he is
likely to leave her with respect both to her future and the
future of the children.

Thus we come to the close of our description of the
various functional types. The description has been necessarily schematic and obviously cannot do justice to the
manifoldness of life. In the formation of personality,
other factors—for example personal development, experiences, occupation milieu, and many others—also play a
big part. Moreover, we have been discussing thus far
only the so-called dominant functions. Actually, people
also make use, as a rule, of an *auxiliary function*, in
order not to confront life too one-sidedly and thus be
able better to master it. This function is usually borrowed from the other axis. Types located on the rational

axis, that is, thinking and feeling types, develop as an auxiliary function, sensation or intuition. Thus there are thinking and feeling types who demonstrate, as an auxiliary function, a well-developed sensory ability; and there are others who possess, as an auxiliary function, a well-developed intuition.

And the same goes for the other two types so that we may distinguish between intuitive and sensory types who make use of thinking as an auxiliary function and others who use feeling as an auxiliary function.

Thus the above-described differentiation between the axes is complicated by the presence of a relatively well-developed auxiliary function. It is often not easy to determine, for example, whether a man who uses thinking and sensation as his means for self-conscious behavior is a thinking type with a well-developed sensory apparatus as an auxiliary function or whether he is a sensory type with a well-developed thinking apparatus as an auxiliary function. Life is after all extraordinarily complex, and we have no right to overlook reality for the sake of the simplicity and comprehensiveness of our systems.

We cannot enter here into all the nuances which result from the existence of this auxiliary function. But, just as a matter of observed fact, let us note that introverted thinking and feeling types are more likely to develop intuition as an auxiliary function, whereas extroverted thinking and feeling types use sensation as an auxiliary function more frequently.

The Developmental Phases of Marriage

> "When the bleak days come, when flaws appear in one or the other of you, do not think of your ill luck, of your unhappiness. Think of God rather, who has long since known all these flaws and who has brought you together precisely because of them, so that you may help each other to correct your flaws. This is the purpose and the task of your coming together."
>
> JEREMIAS GOTTHELF

In the previous chapters we discussed, at considerable length, the frequent occurrence of differences, indeed of hostility, between marriage partners. The conclusion followed inevitably: the danger of misunderstanding, and thus the likelihood of quarrels and strife, is far greater than is normally assumed, in spite of the good will of the mates. In this analysis, we presented the fundamental psychic attitudes (extrovert-introvert) and the mates belonging to the two pairs of types (thinking, feeling, intuitive, and sensory) as if they were irreconcilable opposites. Now we have to attempt significantly to correct this picture.

The types we have portrayed thus far must not under any circumstances be regarded as something static, rigid, forever and ever fixed. On the contrary, the decisive significance of our marriage typology rests precisely upon its inner dynamic. One might even say, with some exaggeration, that the typology is, as it were, self-liquidating, thanks to its dynamic. This apparently paradoxical phenomenon, which one encounters not only in the psychological realm but also in other areas, is really a basic characteristic of anything that is alive. In this case, then, it vouches for the true-to-life, biologically grounded nature of our typology. While we are young, none of the four functions is likely to be unduly developed. Then, gradually, one of them develops into the dominant function. The function which, within our schema, appears at the opposite pole, will be correspondingly suppressed, exiled into the subconscious. It is obvious that thinking will be the clearer and the more objective, the more all show of emotion is eliminated and that, conversely, objective consideration and logical conclusions act as a break upon the intensity and immediacy of feeling. Similarly, sensation and intuition restrain each other, at least at the outset. How could the sensory function be fully developed, unless we concentrated first on whatever might be palpable, accessible to the senses? Thus we always exercise and sharpen that one of the four functions by means of which we attempt to understand and master our world. On the other hand, we banish the counter-function in the same measure to our subconscious where it then becomes the favorite instrument of our "shadow." C. G. Jung designates as "shadow" the sum total of those traits which we possess but which we would rather not acknowledge as belonging to our ego. Thus the "shadow" forms a kind of dark counter-pole to the consciously desired character of our personality. But the "shadow" is by no means something merely negative, as one might perhaps assume. On the contrary, the "shadow" contains many tendencies which might very happily complement our conscious tendencies, provided that these tendencies could be properly developed and duly fitted into the totality of our psyche.

It appears that in every grown man there is some dim awareness of this possibility of complementation and some vague but highly purposeful drive to realize this possibility. Just as we seek bodily complementation through our urge toward that which is different in a member of the other sex, even if we are not yet aware of the nature of this difference nor able to understand our inner drives, even so we find ourselves driven, in the psychic-spiritual realm, toward complementation through contact with our opposite pole.

The majority of people find themselves at this developmental stage when they reach marriageable age or enter into marriage. At this stage, then, the thinking type has more or less severely suppressed his feelings, the feeling type has dealt likewise with his thinking function, and so on. By dint of the drive for complementation which we have just discussed, the thinking type longs greatly for completion through feeling, which he needs. But his own feelings are at this point exiled, undeveloped. Therefore he will not consider them as equal to complementing his well-developed thinking function. But if this thinking type happens to meet a suitable and equally developed feeling type, he will find in her, in flesh and blood form, that which he is basically searching for in himself. There is a remarkable consonance between that which a man is seeking according to his inner need for complementation and the person whom he happens to meet. This consonance seems to be the very basis on which two people fall in love.

It is a familiar phenomenon that lovers always feel they have been destined for each other by fate, that they somehow knew each other in another world. This inner experience is portrayed in a large number of myths of the widest variety of peoples, and we encounter it in our time as much as ever.

In this first phase of the meeting of two persons, the two conscious dominant functions, that is, according to our example, the man's thinking and the woman's feeling, complement each other very well indeed. So do the two subconscious, undeveloped functions, notably the man's undeveloped feeling and the woman's undeveloped thinking. But these two undeveloped functions do not play a large part for the time being. The woman thinks like the man she loves, the man feels like his wife. This phase, however, in which there is such complete identification that one thinks like the other, feels like the other, soon comes to an end. The husband begins again to live by his own feelings, his wife starts doing her own thinking once more. Tensions arise. The undeveloped thinking of the feeling type does not accord with the well-developed thinking of the thinking type—and the same occurs with respect to feelings. Thus differences of opinion and of feeling appear. One may observe this condition ordinarily after the first few years of a previously peaceful and, for the most part, relatively happy marriage.

These arguments between man and wife, that is, between two fundamentally different types, constitute then one of the lasting causes for those tensions in marriage which were dealt with extensively in the previous chapters. Again and again, in every conceivable situation, the mates will come into conflict over the different way in which they experience and work out things. And let us remember that the divergent basic orientation—extrovert-introvert—further reduces the possibility of mutual understanding. Day after day therefore each type will find it necessary to "have things out" with his opposite type. But one of the most important tasks of marriage consists of precisely in this often so labored and painful "having it out." In this phase, it will become evident what the two persons really want to make of their marriage, and that in turn will depend greatly on their concept of the nature of marriage itself. If they are captives of the immature middle-class image of marriage as a happy haven in which one finds rest and a carefree life after the "storms of youth," or if they perceive marriage chiefly as a legalized and tradition-sanctioned arrangement for the risk-free fulfillment of their need for sex and happiness, they will, in this second phase of the development of their marriage, sooner or later find their way to a judge of the Domestic Relations court; or one or the other mate will seek satisfaction outside the marriage, in one form or another. Their marriage will become a kind of shared housing arrangement which they may continue to maintain for the sake of convention or perhaps "for the children's sake," but it will no longer deserve the name of marriage.

Others, at this stage, regard marriage as a cross which

they must bear. They become more or less good-natured martyrs, tolerating each other but neglecting to explore the deeper meaning of their marital crisis. Thus they may have on their hands a permanent crisis, with all its consequences both for them and for their children.

At the outset we claimed that the search for the meaning of such a crisis could be extremely fruitful both for the individuals involved and for the development of their marriage. We would like to quote once more the saying of Hippocrates, according to whom "all illness is both divine and human." Married people who would apply this bit of wisdom to their own "marriage illness" might begin to understand that the stubborn conflicts they are experiencing are not caused exclusively by their respective human imperfections. And if, in addition, each of the mates should begin a search within himself and perhaps gradually discover that some of the very qualities of which he had been particularly proud were most seriously aggravating his relationship with the other, then they might both find themselves in the midst of that psychic transformation which might well have to occur in any authentic marriage sooner or later; and this transformation is essentially the same for a couple as the process of psychic regrouping of the individual which Jung has described as the "life turning point."

In the course of this transformation, we begin to understand that our vaunted logic was perhaps just love-lessness; that our sense of justice was largely contempt for the wishes of our mate; or that our tolerance, of which we were so proud, was more like cowardice and ir-responsibility. Or we might gradually realize that our

relentless solicitude, which our mate rejected as tyran-
nical, was actually not quite as selfless as we had fancied;
or that the even temper, which we managed to show
even in the midst of severe upheavals, actually concealed
far more indifference than we had assumed. But such
insight into the relativity of qualities which up to now
we have so greatly prized simultaneously opens our
eyes to new and hitherto overlooked values both in our
selves and in our mate. We now become able, perhaps
for the first time, to see our wholly different mate as a
new person, to understand him, to let him be himself. At
the same rate as we begin truly to understand our mate,
we will also learn better to value our own hitherto
repressed nature, our "shadow," and we will be able to
bring to consciousness and gradually to develop our
hitherto undeveloped functions. For example, I will
no longer remain a one-sided thinking type with
altogether undifferentiated feelings, but my thinking function will be complemented more and more by a developed, appropriately graded and shaded feeling function.
Similarly, if I have been a one-sided feeling type, my
emotional life will become better ordered, more harmonious, thanks to the gradual development of my thinking
function. If I am a woman, I will now be able to develop
that peculiarly feminine spirituality which men so greatly
prize and always have revered, and which stands in entire
contrast to the "blue stocking," self-righteous intellectual
arrogance of many females who feel obligated to deny
their feminine nature in order to be able to converse
with men.

Similarly, the sensory type will be developing his intuitive function. This will lead to a growing appreciation of meaning relationships, to greater serenity and greater faith in the future, and to a certain openness toward the religious and the mystical. And this attitude will effectively complement his prior attitude of excessive preoccupation with utility or aesthetics. The intuitive type in his turn will be coming closer to reality. The world-estranged enthusiast will gradually turn into a reality-oriented person, conscious of his responsibility and enjoying it. Thus the mates will develop with respect to each other. And the more mature they become, the better they will be able to understand each other. Now they are ready to let each other live. More than that: the difference of my mate will now produce an animating and creative tension in me; and if there remains something in him which defies my understanding, at least I will be able to respect it. It will now be possible to appreciate and cheerfully follow the remark of Hattingberg: "To love a person means to see him as God would have him."

This "rounding out" in the development of the personality of the individual, which we have been describing, is known in modern psychology as "individuation." There exists also for the marriage organism, the married couple, a corresponding level of development, which I would like to designate as the third developmental phase in marriage.

From the first stage of a loving but unconscious I-I relationship—passing through a stage of conscious but objective, matter-of-fact I-it relationship—we now have genuine community, a conscious and loving I-thou encounter.

PART TWO

"We regard the mutual inner formation of the spouses, their persistent effort to lead each other toward completeness, as properly speaking the chief ground and the deepest meaning of marriage."

Encyclical *Casti Conubii*

In the first part of this book we demonstrated how marriage partners differ in important respects in the great majority of marriages. From these differences in their fundamental attitude toward life and toward the world tensions and conflict necessarily result. We noted repeatedly that it is desirable and necessary to develop a calm, objective, even benevolent stance toward this psychological difference of one's mate, and that, by so doing, it is possible to prevent many difficulties which might create conflict in the marriage. Such an attitude toward the mate eventually leads to the point where the difference is no longer experienced as disturbing and irritating, but rather as invigorating and downright exciting. Thus new creative forces are awakened in the marriage, and the inner life of the marriage organism is restored.

Thus far we have limited our discussion exclusively to the typological differences of the marriage partners. Now, however, it is necessary to discuss those *sexually* conditioned essential differences between man and woman which, though easier to understand, are no less significant. Here again, just as in the case of the typological differences, we are dealing with peculiarities of the partners which are grounded in their very being, which therefore occur in every marriage and are thus likely to create tensions and conflicts in every marriage. Of course, it is rather artificial to sort out the typological from the sexually conditioned psychological traits of any individual. In real life, they are closely interwoven. Thus, in order to create greater clarity in this complicated department of psychology, it has been necessary to describe separately the two main forms in which differences in the basic traits of marriage partners occur.

The Sexual-Erotic Differences Between Man and Woman

The sexual-erotic differences between marriage partners involve of course a great deal more than the difference in their sexual organs or the different tasks which are theirs in connection with the begetting of children. Nevertheless, these bodily differences themselves are a particularly conspicuous expression of the incompleteness of the individual. In order to bring to birth a child, which is something new, something that points beyond the individual, cooperation of the true whole is necessary. And this applies to the physical as well as to the psychological dimension.

Bodily differences and emotional differences, how-

ever, do not affect marriage in the same way. The reason
for this difference is that most people, by the time they
are married, have attained a certain physical maturity
so that their respective physical endowments naturally
complement and fulfill each other. In the emotional
realm, however, such maturity is rarely present at the
time of marriage. It is true that most mates are sufficiently
developed psychologically at the outset of their marriage
that it is possible to speak of the relatively complementary nature of their emotional differences. Seldom, however, are both of them fully matured personalities at this
point. Only in marriage and—if they understand the
nature of marriage correctly—*through* marriage, will they
develop gradually to that level of maturity. For this reason, physical harmony is so much easier and more
natural to achieve than spiritual harmony. What are the
respective sexual-erotic orientations of man and woman?
How do they experience their sexuality, and how does
it operate in their everyday existence rather than just in
the brief moments of bodily union?

Man's sexual tension rises, from a neutral point
zero, suddenly and to a very high level. It rapidly achieves
its highest intensity and demands release. When release
is obtained, man quickly descends once again to a sexual-
erotic zero point. And there he remains, until a new,
brusque ascent occurs. Between these peaks, man is, as
it were, "empty of love" for a longer or shorter time.
During such a neutral interim, he is relatively free
erotically. In this phase, therefore, he is able to con-
centrate on factual or spiritual matters, to take an interest
in things from which sexual love is wholly excluded. For

example, he will engage in scientific work, solve intellectual or technical problems, in short, pursue his occupation. And this he is able to do without any regard whatever for his wife, entirely absorbed and fulfilled in his vocation, his work. The expression "without regard" may be taken quite literally in this case, in that he will hardly cast a glance in the direction of his wife, whereas she, who wants to be noticed more than anything else, will fare rather ill under such treatment. For she depends very much on the attention and consideration of her husband. If he pays no attention to her she will find him inconsiderate, and cruelly so.

The love graph of a woman follows an entirely different design. Once her love is awakened, it remains ever wakeful. She never sinks all the way to that zero point. For a woman, love is here to stay. It rises more gradually toward its peak, and, upon release, its descent is also more gradual. But it never descends as far as does the love graph of a man. A woman's erotic feeling is always present, at least to a degree. Therefore there is nothing purely objective, purely scientific, purely businesslike for her. Whatever she does, she does it always for her husband or for her children or for other people. It is for them she cooks, cleans, washes, mends clothes. It is for them that she decorates herself and her home. Therefore she cannot really understand why her husband does not respond to this love, why he hardly even notices her. It is very natural for her to talk often about her love, to ask her husband anxiously, "Do you still love me?" This sad question expresses her astonishment at the fact that her husband is able, at certain times, to exist without love, that at times he is, as it were, absent from this love, that he is able to be cool and objective.

The difference which we have just described appears in countless everyday marital difficulties. It leads to tensions and, if the partners do not recognize the fundamental nature of the difference, to a feeling of misunderstanding which will put a heavy burden upon the marriage organism. Let us illustrate with a very ordinary example.

On a certain morning, the husband has a brief exchange of words with his wife over some trifle, just before he leaves for work. When he comes home for lunch, the atmosphere is calmer but harmony has not yet been clearly and consciously restored. At night, he comes home from work in a very good mood. He is in high spirits, amiable, affectionate toward his wife. He has long since forgotten the little morning incident. In the course of the evening, he wants to have intimate contact with his wife, but he encounters a resistance which he finds wholly incomprehensible and wounding.

Why does his wife remain cool or downright negative? Why does she not allow herself to be infected by his good mood and inner satisfaction? What has come over her, anyway? These are questions the husband asks himself, and, from his standpoint, he seems to be quite right.

The woman, especially if she happens to belong to the introverted type, is in such cases similarly amazed at her husband's conduct. More precisely, his conduct saddens her, because this scene has been played so often that she has ceased being amazed. But she still cannot understand how her husband can be so indifferent and loveless. How is it possible that he should have forgotten what happened this morning? The woman feels and thinks, "That argument of this morning is still between us; something more has to be done about it to restore harmony."

From the husband's point of view, the wife's feelings appear petty: she is far too sensitive, too easily bruised. Where is that much-vaunted feminine readiness to give oneself freely, to forgive graciously? After all, *he* has been friendly and affectionate. He has proved, by his speech and actions, that the morning incident has become a thing of the past. For him, feelings are just not so important and decisive.

But for his wife this is not enough, and this is rather typical of women. The relationship of love which was disturbed in the morning has not yet been restored. And she cannot simply get over her sense of disharmony. It is impossible for her truly to consent to sexual union as long as marital harmony is lacking. The husband thinks that sexual union is the very thing that will take care of whatever residue of disharmony there may be. For his wife, however, such a notion is incomprehensible. She is unable to give herself unreservedly to her husband as long as she does not feel spiritually at one with him; and for that she needs at least a little talk about the incident of the morning. Any attempt to restore sexual togetherness before recovering their emotional erotic unity strikes her as crude, indeed as animalistic. Above all, she disapproves of the incomprehensible indifference of her husband who, in his conduct, demonstrates so little awareness of her feminine nature, which demands that he take such incidents with due seriousness, because they strike her as serious.

The attentive reader can readily imagine that the scene we have just described is most likely to occur in marriages where the man is extroverted and the woman is introverted. Should the woman happen to be an introverted feeling type, unable to project her feelings, her bad mood would be particularly easy for her husband to overlook. In that case he would experience her recalcitrance as particularly unexpected and incomprehensible, as a silly mood or as something having to do with the weather—that most frequently accused scapegoat. As an extrovert, it will not even occur to him that he himself may have a part in the present disharmony. He has just spent an entire day adapting himself to the moods of those around him. Therefore he cannot believe that anyone could hang on to a bad morning mood as late as evening, when he himself has lived through so much in the course of the day. To the introverted wife, however, this seems obvious, because feelings are very important for her, especially if she happens to be a feeling type. She lives with her feelings and by her feelings. To her, it seems fickle and superficial simply to give up a feeling, as her husband is able to do, just because the environment happens to have been differently attuned. The husband, in his turn, judges her conduct as grudge bearing, though it is simply the result of her introversion.

Such an incident, insignificant in itself, pushes the woman emotionally off balance, because for her, her relationship with her husband is by far the most im-

portant thing in the world. She has spent the whole day
alone, in the company of her disturbed love relationship.
Why should she fix food, when her husband barely pays
attention to it? Why should she clean the house when
none of these things really matter to her husband?

She says, "none of these things," and she means just
that, because, for her, everything is disturbed when her
love relationship is disturbed. Her husband, however,
shakes his head, uncomprehendingly, and says to himself,
"How can my wife take such little things so seriously?
How can she doubt my love because of such trifles?" He
goes to work, surrenders himself wholeheartedly to the
problems of his profession, and therefore quite normally
forgets what to him seems to be such a little thing—the
morning episode. How can a woman make so much of
a little thing, over against all the misery and all the
responsibilities which he encounters in his daily work?
This is how his thoughts are likely to run after he has
at last learned from his wife, following a midnight discussion, why she had refused to give herself to him.

The different way in which a man and a woman
experience life colors their entire marriage. For the man,
sexual union is an event with a significance of its own,
having its own independent experiential value. Through
sexual intercourse, he is able to recover community after
having spent some time in a certain emotional isolation,
a certain erotic neutrality, for example, after the day's
work. This feeling of belonging, restored by the sexual
event, he now takes with him joyfully, and he proceeds
to discharge the energy he has accumulated from being
with his wife, in his work. He is now able to perform with

heightened creativity and new zest, because his work now seems ever so much more meaningful to him. It is for this reason that a man is able to attribute a spiritual meaning to sexual union, indeed a metaphysical significance.

The woman's story is entirely different. For the feminine soul, sexual union is both less and more. It is something very close and palpable. Her spiritual surrender is directed far more precisely at the person of her husband, perhaps at the hoped-for child. A woman expects every sexual union to bring her closer to her husband and to remain closer to him ever after.

An hour of peaceful togetherness in which the woman knows that her husband is really beside her, an hour during which he really participates in everything she tells him and he tells her, is likely to mean a great deal more to most women than any stormy sexual encounter, during which she loves her husband, to be sure, but in which her husband actually gives himself to the experience rather than to his wife.

The Erotic Misunderstanding

Insofar as a man is rather directly excitable, he is likely to interpret his wife's need to cling to him, her groping for friendliness and protection, as heralds of sexual activity. But for the woman this does not by any means follow. Her need for tenderness may be wholly free from sexual desire, so free indeed that she may recoil in fright when she senses that her husband is responding with sexual desire. Both husband and wife ought to acquaint themselves with these fundamental differences between men and women if they would avoid constant misunderstandings. Young men are in special danger of falling prey to this so-called erotic misunderstanding. They tend to believe all too readily that they must prove their virility, when only tenderness and chivalry may be expected.

This erotic misunderstanding, that is to say, the tendency to advance toward sexual contact in a situation in which attentiveness and tenderness are called for, occurs frequently nowadays, especially among younger men. This may be related in large part to the widespread though partly misunderstood sexual enlightenment of our age. Young people, single or married, often tell us how they thought that, in a particular situation, sexual union was expected to occur. But the very fact that they entertain this thought instead of experiencing the situation, that they feel in a sense obligated to engage in sexual intercourse, as if they were dealing with a rule of etiquette they were obligated to observe, proves that they would do better to contain themselves.

The situation we have just described demonstrates one of the evil consequences of the overdevelopment of the thinking function which has been observed in many men and which we dealt with in Part I. This overdevelopment of the thinking function, we noted, takes its toll in terms of the underdevelopment of the feeling function and the sensory function. Such men tend to reveal an astonishing uncertainty of instinct. They are unable to act as spontaneously and naturally as more primitive or intellectually less developed men are able.

Introverted men are aware of this uncertainty in themselves and experience it painfully; indeed—as was noted in the description of the introverted thinking type —they appear ridiculous to themselves and are therefore likely to avoid such encounters, indeed to avoid women altogether. Extroverts, on the other hand, are naive enough to believe that the exercise of their sexual vigor will particularly endear them to their beloved. C. G. Jung comments: "Most men are erotically blind in that they commit the unpardonable error of confusing Eros with sexuality. A man thinks that he possesses a woman when he is possessing her sexually. But never is he possessing her less, because for the woman only the erotic relationship is truly significant. For her, marriage is a relationship, and sexuality an addendum."[1]

Man's uncertainty of instinct and his temptation to avoid an encounter for which he feels inadequate are of course dysfunctional from the standpoint of the basically desirable coming together of the sexes. Here a woman who is sure of her instincts and close to nature can come to the aid of the man in the most matter-of-fact and natural way, especially if she is a feeling type or a sensory type. If she is a real woman, that is, a true daughter of Eve, she will know how to help him without letting him know that he is being helped: she will gladly

[1] C. G. Jung, *Women in Europe* (Zurich: Rascher, 1932).

let him believe that he is the conqueror when, in reality, he has been seduced. And she will not have to feel that she is putting on an act when she is acting in this way. For a woman, there is actually nothing false in this conduct. But if we try to explain this, in the course of marriage counseling, to an all too sober and intellectual woman, she will indignantly decline to engage in play-acting. And by her very objection, she demonstrates how far she has wandered from her original and natural feminine being.

When a man finds out about the skillful behavior of a woman in such a situation, he is amazed: partly fascinated, partly alarmed. He is likely to ask himself afterward whether it is the woman's scheming or her naive innocence which has caused things to work out so well.

But we cannot describe the woman's action as "scheming," if by that we mean a conscious and purposeful stratagem which is only apparently guileless and transparent. And we cannot describe her action as "naive" if by that we mean a truly simpleminded, pristine, unconscious, and altogether passive conduct. The very words, "scheming" and "naive," proceed from a purely masculine outlook and therefore do not really apply to a woman. They assume that purposeful behavior must necessarily be conscious, whereas unconscious behavior is more likely passive behavior, and cannot in any case have a purposeful character. This just does not happen to be true of the feminine psyche. One might almost say, by contrast, that women act the more purposefully, the more unconsciously they are acting. Having stated the paradox, let us formulate it somewhat more in detail. Women "scheme" most effectively when they are not "scheming" at all. Insofar as they have remained sure of their instincts, they do not need to be conscious of their purposes in order to act purposefully, since it is well known that there is hardly anything more purposeful than instinct. But it would not be entirely correct, either, to suggest that women are in such moments totally unconscious. As a rule they know pretty well what it is they really want. However, they do not choose the means to their ends on the basis of conscious reflection, but they entrust themselves to their "nature" which then assists them in obtaining the desired results with a combination of seemingly naive naturalness and seemingly scheming purposefulness.

Mutual Appreciation in Marriage

> "We women are not complete beings, and you
> men are no more complete than we are. How
> can we hope to accomplish anything grand or
> beautiful without helping one another?"
>
> SELMA LAGERLOF

For a man, the most significant thing in life is his work, his objective accomplishment. His work emerges gradually in some permanent and lasting form, and he feels himself affirmed by his creation. This feeling is clearly and understandably expressed in his professional pride. In addition, he expects regular material recognition of his work in the form of money.

For a woman, especially for a housewife, the situation is as a rule very different. Her devotion to her work appears in the form of clean, well-scrubbed children and a husband in neat, well-cared-for clothes, in the form of loving care for these and other persons. Unlike her husband she does not normally receive any external recognition for her work in the form of regular pay. Nevertheless, she also has a quite natural need to be appreciated and to have her efforts and worries met with understanding. And this is something which men seldom realize. Time and again, a husband could cheer up his wife with just a few friendly, appreciative words. He could help her to enjoy or at least to endure her often thankless house-work.

Conversely, a man is highly receptive to any expression of appreciation by his wife. He is not as likely to expect his wife to admire him for his professional activity. More likely, he looks for some praise of his particular "manly virtues" and of his excellence in such pursuits as may occupy his leisure time as hobbyist, sportsman, "artist"—of his "amateur" accomplishments. Men are likely to be particularly proud of such gifts. In these areas, in which the activity is not entirely serious, they often react somewhat childishly by wanting to be praised like little boys.

But it is not enough simply to accept the work of a woman without giving her any "buildup." A woman has a deep and legitimate need for some appreciation, some real understanding, by her husband. Any appreciation she does not feel is as unreal to a woman as a salary he is not receiving is to a man.

This entirely legitimate but often unfulfilled desire for some recognition is a frequent, unconscious source of marital disturbances. If a woman does not feel adequately understood and appreciated, she will be tempted to compensate for the missing understanding by securing the attention, if not the esteem, of her husband. If her positive accomplishments cannot induce her husband to turn toward her—if the care of her beauty no longer entices him from his world into her world—she will often seek other means in order to establish contact with him. Perhaps she will begin to dress conspicuously or to act so as to attract the attention of other men in order to make her husband jealous. Or she will force him through physical sickness or weakness to pay attention to her and in this way to be near her, at least outwardly.

By means of such behavior, a woman imperceptibly enters that area of pathological reactions which the specialist calls hysteria. Many scenes and "acts" which husbands usually put down with a contemptuous wave of the hand as feminine theatrics have to be judged and treated from this viewpoint. So does much steady complaining about fatigue, headaches, migraines, dizziness, backaches, and abdominal cramps. Such complaints and ailments are simple signals—signals to the man. They mean: "Don't leave me to myself! Pay attention to me! Understand me! Be near me!" If men could only develop into better psychologists and more attentive husbands, they would not have to pay so many medical bills. They would not have to send their wives to so many hospitals and spas. They would not have to show such complicated consideration for their unpredictable and constantly changing problems. With just a few cheering and appreciative words, with just a little time devoted daily to their wives, they would have it within their power to transform these complaining, sickly, sullen persons into friendly, gay, joyful creatures. Of course, more is involved here than just to raise the head slightly from the newspaper and to listen, with patent reluctance, to whatever gossip and small nothings the woman may have to offer. No, it is necessary to pay real attention, to make it very clear to her that her problems of household or child rearing, her troubles with maids and neighbors, are important matters in a homemaker's world, since they involve the order and peace of her domain.

Women, on the other hand, should be equally aware of the connection between their feeling of neglect by their husbands and their many physical and emotional troubles. They should realize that complaints about migraine headaches or backaches are not a good means for awakening the interest of their husbands in their problems and wishes. It would be far better for a woman to talk with her husband once, or if necessary, more than once, in order to make it clear to him that she is suffering from his lack of interest and sympathetic concern. In addition, every woman should strive to develop her own intellectual capacities. She should make every effort to outgrow the all too narrow circle of her household and familial cares—to participate in some of the larger communities—to develop an interest in social, artistic, and religious questions, and to maintain this interest within her marriage. Such an intellectually alive woman will be less dependent upon her husband's appreciation. She will measure her everyday problems with a different yardstick and will thus be able to remain calmer and more joyful even when the harmony of her marriage and family life is temporarily marred by disagreements. The conditions for achieving an understanding with her husband are far more propitious for this woman than they are for another who is totally submerged in the care of household and family. Furthermore, an intellectually alert woman will understand her husband's mode of thinking better and will be able to communicate her concerns to him more clearly and impressively. We thus come back, by a slightly different route, to a bit of advice which we dealt with extensively in Part I, namely, that we should develop our counter-function in order to be able better to understand our mate. In the case of a woman, this would mean developing her ability to think matter-of-factly, objectively, rather than remaining imprisoned in the narrow sphere of her immediate tasks. And experience proves that women who allow themselves to be totally submerged in their everyday concerns eventually lose any real understanding of the personal needs of their husband and of their children as well.

Such women experience their exaggerated wifely and maternal concerns as a kind of emotional "idling." The thrust of their energy will be directed at clean floors and a spic and span kitchen rather than at the people who live in the house. Such a mind-set cannot produce gratitude and appreciation. At best, it will produce sympathy for so much exaggerated solicitude. More likely, it will produce anger and disagreement. For such exaggerated solicitude is often a kind of concealed tyranny: a tyranny of love, to be sure, but nevertheless a tyranny. Such a woman may say, "We like an old-fashioned house," and the family must live in an old-fashioned house. Or she will say, "We enjoy bland food," and the family must eat bland food. Or, again, "We don't like to go out in the evening," and no one goes out in the evening—at least for a time. Gradually, however, the husband begins to defend himself against this loving vassalage, and the children soon follow suit. And if the woman does not realize where her exaggerated solicitude is leading, her husband will be defending himself more and more savagely against her encroachments. Or else he will be trying to escape his wife's excessive mothering of him by means of all kinds of pretexts.

Mother or Wife?

Behind this question that we pose, in exaggerated form, as an alternative, there is a problem which appears in many marriages and which, I am sure, causes more difficulties in Switzerland than anywhere else. I have in mind the attitude of women toward motherhood. Motherhood and motherliness are rightfully among the most highly prized values of culture. However, while being properly appreciative of them, we dare not forget that there is also something instinctual, something unruly about them.

It is well known that woman's reproductive instinct is only in part of a sexual nature. In part, it is maternal. And in many women, this maternal part far outweighs the sexual part. In man, on the other hand, the paternal instinct plays a far less important part within his sexual drive. Thus, when a husband learns that his wife is expecting, he is probably able to understand, intellectually, how significant this fact is for him and for his marriage. He is about to become father of a family. But at first all this remains somehow outside his person. The importance of the event enters his consciousness primarily through its effects upon his young wife. And, just now, when his wife is going through such a profound and vitally significant experience, he can do little more than accompany her, at a distance, with his sympathetic concern. Only in this indirect way is he able to participate in the enormous transformation which motherhood is effecting in the body and soul of his wife.

The woman, on the other hand, is being preoccupied more and more by motherhood. She is inclined to forget that, for her husband, she is still above all his wife. And she begins to leave him to his own devices more and more, even if she does not want to, even if she tries consciously to fight the tendency. She is no longer able to marshal the proper feeling for his dissatisfaction, because her feelings are no longer available to her husband to the extent they used to be. More and more, her feelings are drawn to her child. And, in extreme cases, they come to be centered entirely on her child.

This shifting of the woman's feeling to the child and the inevitably related withdrawal of her feelings from her husband do not stop at the birth of the child; it extends far into the nursing period. Then the young mother begins gradually to turn once again toward her husband and to feel more like a wife, so that the development of the man-woman relationship, interrupted at the onset of pregnancy, regains its intensity.

Frequently, however, the mysterious changes which occur not only in the body but also in the psyche of a woman during pregnancy result in a new *permanent* attitude toward her husband. A woman with a childish or undeveloped sexuality or one who hasn't found much satisfaction in married life for other reasons is particularly prone to use the experience of motherhood, though unconsciously, as a means of flight from her husband. Often she is unconsciously guided by the intention to remove herself in this way from any confrontation with him. And this applies as much to purely sexual relations as it does to the more spiritual aspects of the marriage relationship.

Any woman who limits herself to such a degree to being a mother necessarily estranges her husband. No longer does she exhibit for his specifically masculine interest, let alone to his professional and spiritual concerns, that sympathetic concern which is essential to a working marriage.

Small wonder that such a husband begins to look around for another woman, that he seeks somehow to supplement his mother-wife with a "comrade." But few wives have any idea to what extent they burden their marriage and drive their husband into temptation by being bogged down in their instinctual-maternal mindset.

And if such a woman concentrates her remaining energy exclusively on perfect housekeeping, if she continues to function as a good cook and housekeeper for her husband but no longer as his mate and comrade, her marriage is likely to be threatened by a severe inner crisis. The particular difficulty of this kind of a marriage situation lies in the fact that the wife is usually entirely unaware of the extent to which her own conduct promotes her husband's forthcoming unfaithfulness and the general undermining of their marriage.

On the basis of appearances, a man in such a marriage has perhaps little ground for complaint. But the inside view is very different—and this is demonstrated by extensive experience in marriage counseling. The husband suffers from the homely ways of his wife more than he realizes. Only when he notices his proneness to temptation—upon meeting a woman who may be more frivolous but less sober of thought, more intellectually stimulating, and more oriented toward him—only then does he realize how much he has been missing the feminine charm and grace of his own wife-turned-mother.

Now it may happen, at this stage of development, that the woman becomes aware of her husband's potential or accomplished unfaithfulness. But if she begins to worry, if she no longer wants him to go out by himself, if she becomes jealous and suspicious as soon as she sees him in conversation with another woman, she is not counteracting the unfavorable development of the marriage: rather, she is accelerating it. For now the man begins, in return, to avoid his wife and to stay away from the house under all manner of pretexts. His home appears confining to him, perhaps a prison. He longs to get away from the excessive mothering and solicitude of his all too motherly wife. He yearns for adventure— and the adventure may turn out to be a sexual adventure.

What man indeed could guarantee that he would never, even in thought or wish, incur such guilt? And should the wife, when she senses something of this sort in her husband, insist upon her legal rights? Should she set herself up as the judge of her no doubt guilty and straying but perhaps misunderstood husband? No one could forbid her to do so, since she is defending her home and her children! But Maria Waser, one of the finest representatives of womanhood, has bequeathed to us, in her unforgettable Saffa-Lecture, a few remarkable words about the attitude of the woman who finds herself in this extremity. And if the thrust of her address is directed at the attitude of a mother toward her growing son, it is clear that the basic attitude which she describes in poetic words also applies to the truly feminine attitude of a woman toward her husband. "She (the wife and mother) knows that his (the man or the son) ways are not close to the earth like ours, that they rather thrust him forward into the perilous unknown. . . . And how vulnerable he is in spite of his strength, because nature did not make him calm and gay and self-giving, but rather self-willed, restless, driven by hidden fires, instinctively pressing toward goals ever unattainable, always capable of change—and how he simply cannot wait or be still or grow old. A mother must know how hard it is for a man who has not experienced life-in-the-making to believe in this life and in its fulfillment. It is her task therefore to dissolve his little faith in her great faith. We have to impart to him our knowledge of the holy life, our faith in the holy life, not by lecturing but by being—by our attitude toward him—by our spiritual going-with-him, our changeless persistence, our steadfast devotion, our faith in him and in his calling; yes by all these things which are comprised in the single concept—love!"

How little is said here about activity and action! "Not by lecturing but by being—by persistence—by devotion," says Maria Waser. If women only knew how many men long for this truly feminine-mother attitude! Many a man would inwardly return to his wife to whom he is now bound by a mere external bond! He might at last find in his own marriage that security which he has been seeking, perhaps restlessly and unhappily, in a thousand activities and distractions.

And may I quote one more sentence from the Saffa-Lecture of Maria Waser because it calls attention to one task of a woman which cannot be stressed enough: "Feminine hands have, from time immemorial, lighted Christmas trees, filled gardens with flowers and even transformed cemeteries into joyful gardens. . . . So much joy are we able to give when we have once again found ourselves." Here Maria Waser speaks of joy, of the sense of duty, of the potential we have for growing beyond what is merely utilitarian, useful, and necessary. In this realm, we find the things that make us truly human, the things that make us into creatures capable of outgrowing ourselves and finding meaning in our existence so that we may willingly submit ourselves to a higher order of things. And if we are convinced that in this higher order of things everything makes sense, even misery and suffering, we will be ready to accept even these aspects of life in a manner characteristic of men of faith who can afford to be serene and joyful, because their faith assures them that, ultimately, they are being sustained by a gracious hand.

Some Advice
for Better Marriages

*"Those who have never hurt each other have
never loved each other."*
                              CHARLES TSCHOPP

In conclusion and, in a way, as a practical summary
of everything that has been said so far, we want to return
once more to the everyday realities of marriage and to
discuss some of the specifics of better and more effective
conduct in marriage in the form of three words of advice
gleaned from experience.

The first word of advice is, "Learn to fight!" This
bit of advice may well appear surprising but if you are
ready to follow it, you may experience new life and
harmony in your marriage.

What then is involved in this right kind of fighting?
First of all the insight that differences of viewpoints between mates are unavoidable. This is something we have
discussed at considerable length. In the second place,
this bit of advice suggests that we learn how to state our
differences of viewpoint correctly. What this means,
mainly, is that we must listen, patiently and benevolently
—that we must let our mate finish. A good listener tries
really to understand the other, to put himself in his
place. He does not keep throwing up to the other his
clumsily chosen but by no means malicious words.
Rather, he recognizes the real meaning and intention of
the statements and accepts them for examination, in a

spirit of goodwill. He does not answer, "But you said . . ." Rather he holds onto what was meant, though it was perhaps poorly said.

Attentive listening also clarifies our own understanding and makes it easier for us to express our response with clarity. Thus a mere fight is elevated to the level of what Häberlin calls "fight conversation." The partners know very well that they are of different opinions, but they are not forgetting that they are striving toward a common goal, notably community. Therefore they will not petulantly assault each other, but they will fight like wise people who know that they will be able to come to terms. Their "fight conversation" will be illuminated by a certain inner joy and trust. And if some genuine, kindly humor begins to appear in their "fight conversation," they are really moving in the right direction. They have learned how to fight properly, and this gives them, in the face of all future differences of opinion, a certain calm and confidence. Now they know that over and above all their differences, they have something in common which is stronger than anything that may threaten to divide them.

The second bit of advice is, "*Learn the art of reconciliation!*" Reconciliation holds a very important place in any good marriage. Even the selection of the proper moment for an attempt at reconciliation is important. Some people find each other again rather quickly. For others, it takes longer for the clouds of ill feeling to drift away. Hanselmann's counsel is, "Whoever recovers his clear and sunny mood first, let him shine and radiate warmth." Big words and gestures are, as a rule, harmful.

Forced and premature ceremonies of reconciliation are equally dangerous. They are foredoomed to failure, if the other is not yet ready to be reconciled. And such a failure pushes even the partner who is ready and willing to be reconciled right back into a bad and defiant mood. Reconciliation demands stillness. It is word-shy. If it is easier for you to find the liberating word and to restore good rapport, do not "push"; watch your timing. Above all, such moments are not designed for a neat distribution of rights and wrongs. The best you can do is to demonstrate to your partner your willingness to be reconciled and your desire for community. This, however, hardly calls for any words at all.

The third bit of advice is, *"Grant your partner more freedom!"* Young married people have a tendency unduly to adapt themselves one to the other. After a while then, one or the other begins to suffer from this excessive adaptation, because he has been forced into patterns or has borrowed opinions which are not true to his real self. Thus tensions arise—a feeling of restriction, of imprisonment, is being experienced.

If such feelings remain unheeded or unconscious, they will lead to all manner of difficulties. It would indeed be an abuse of love in marriage if one of the mates demanded that the other should adapt his entire way of life, at the price of his personal uniqueness. And such uniqueness, as a rule, has little to do with either love or character. It is therefore entirely useless to burden the marriage with the elimination of such differences. It is more helpful to try, as a first step, to make a success of the marriage in spite of the differences. It really comes down to respecting the personality of the other, to letting him be what he is. It is precisely in such things that genuine goodness is revealed, which the other mate will appreciate far more than mere equal rights. And if he feels free from all external pressures, he will try all the more honorably to adapt himself to his mate as much as possible.

It is good to be circumspect and to prepare for marriage; but once the decisive step is taken, it is necessary to go ahead resolutely and wholeheartedly. At that point, we should be able to say to ourselves, with the French author Alin: "Up to now I have been trying to find a person who would please me. From now on, I will try to please the person I found."

A genuine marriage is not a purchase agreement which one may cancel, nor a contract which one may dissolve at will. Whoever enters marriage in this frame of mind puts a heavy mortgage on the house of his marriage from the start. Only he who enters marriage with the firm resolve to stand by his partner with absolute faithfulness, in the good days as well as in the bad days, only he is worthy of the high challenge of marriage.

But if you are casting sidelong glances at the Judge even while you are saying yes, if you reckon that the marriage may easily be terminated if the necessity arises, you are not only entering your marriage frivolously; you are also decisively weakening the marriage you have entered, from its first day. To approach marriage in this frame of mind is to pretend that mutual loyalty and mutual adaptation of the partners is a *gift* of nature. But, quite to the contrary, this is the very task of marriage! On the other hand, if you exclude the very possibility of divorce in advance as something unworthy of consideration, you are likely to exhibit a very different attitude toward even the earthiest of marriage realities. Your attitude, I say, will be very different from the attitudes of another person who keeps flirting with divorce while being forever afraid of divorce, if he happens to be the "injured party." If you know in advance that only death can separate you from mate, you will not be deeply troubled by every instant of conflict, nor will your basic loyalty to your mate be shaken. Rather, any difficulty in the marriage will appear, from the outset, as something temporary. In such a marriage, tensions are passing disturbances to be conquered by common effort rather than convulsions which can shatter the marriage.

In this frame of mind, the day's burden becomes easier to bear, in that it will be regarded as something entirely natural. Such an attitude may even enable you to mitigate, through steadfast effort, the disturbing influence which your mate—who may be a difficult person, chronically ill, or even psychopathic—may have upon your marriage and family. And with such patience, perseverance, and inner strength even the totally unexpected may come to pass: a miraculous transformation of the apparently "incurable" mate may take place! Such inner strength, of course, presupposes a strong, unshakable faith. Under the rays of a truly living faith all possible difficulties and causes for conflicts may, in some inconceivable way, melt and vanish. A living faith is able, even today, to make the impossible possible. For married love becomes endowed with an ultimate, diamond-like glow only when it is irradiated and illuminated, far beyond anything human, by the light of eternity.